My First Picture Dictionary

Coloring & Activity Book

KAPPA LEARNING

Weightless: Being so light you float around in the air

Cactus: A desert plant with pointy spines on the leaves

Turtle: A slow moving reptile, with a shell, that lives in and near the water

 KAPPA Books

Visit us at www.kappapublishing.com/kappabooks

apples
A round, fleshy fruit. Can be green, yellow or red.

armor
A protective body covering.

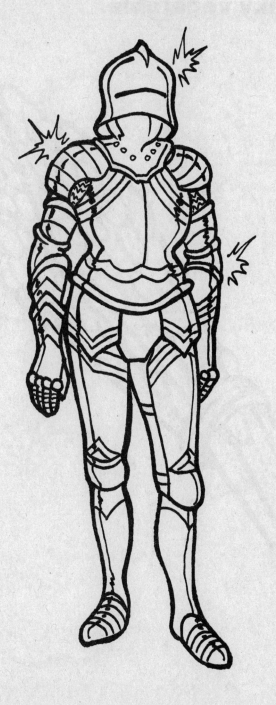

asparagus
A green, spiky vegetable.

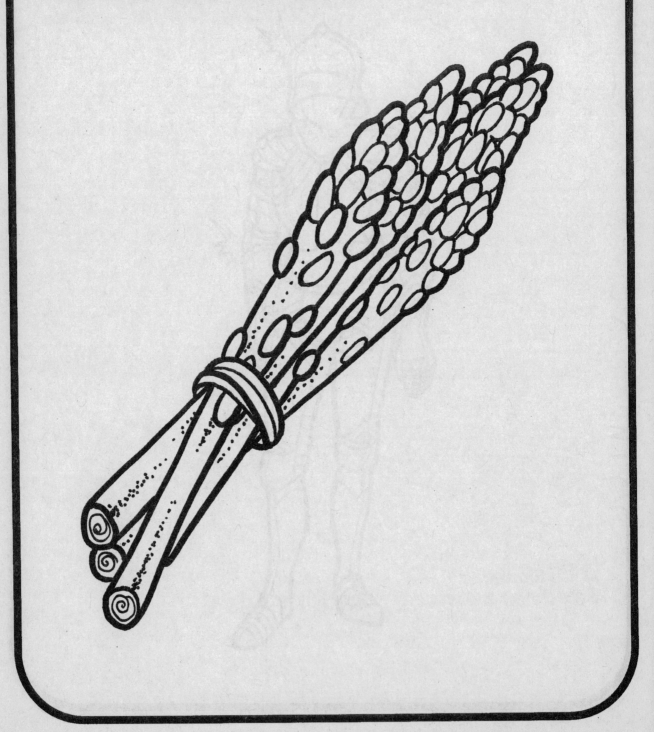

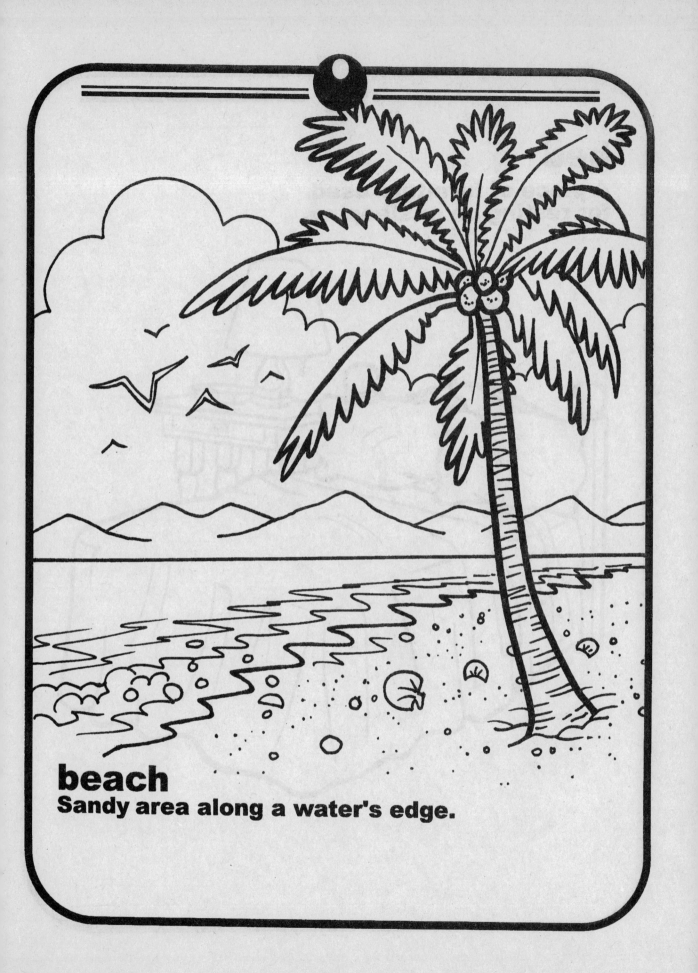

beach
Sandy area along a water's edge.

bed

A piece of furniture used for resting on or sleeping.

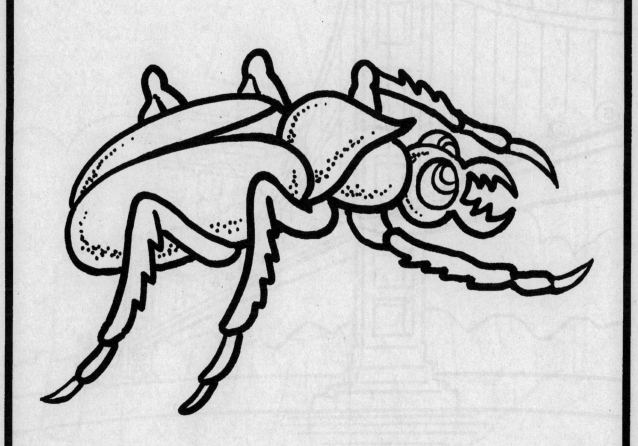

beetle
A biting insect with hard, protective wings.

bridge
A structure built to
connect two places.

campfire
Outdoor fire at a campsite.

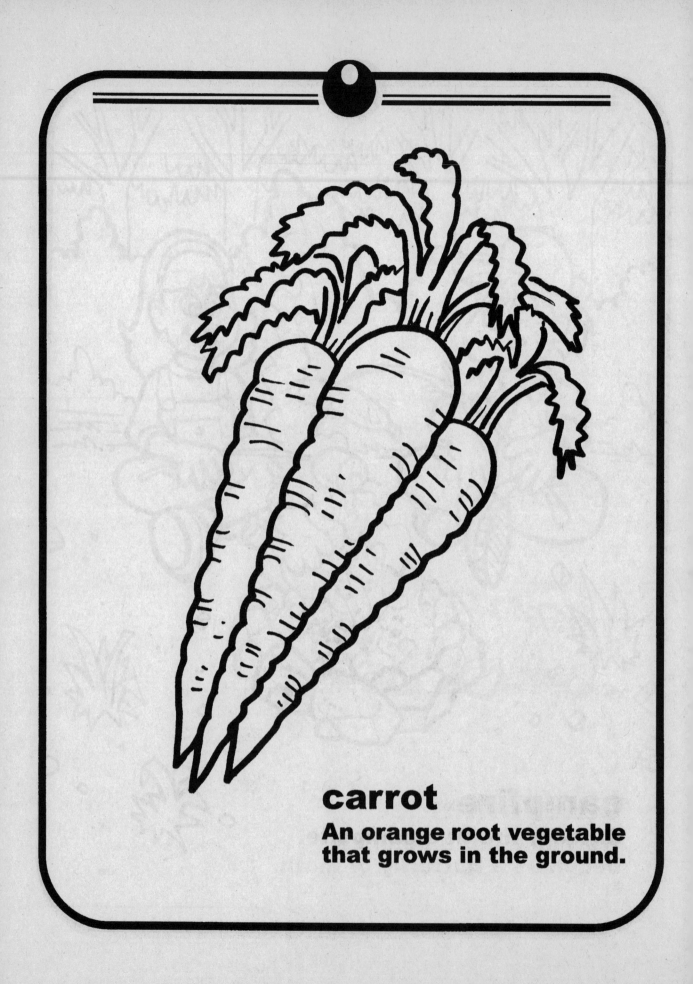

carrot

An orange root vegetable that grows in the ground.

caterpillar
Wormlike larva before it becomes a butterfly or moth.

crab

A crustacean with four pairs of legs, a flat shell and a pair of pincers.

dinosaur
A large, ancient reptile that is now extinct.

dog
A four-legged animal that is kept as a pet.

dolphin
A mammal that lives in the water.

duck

A swimming bird with a flat beak and webbed feet.

dump truck
A truck that is made to carry and dump dirt and other things.

earmuffs

Covering used to keep your ears warm.

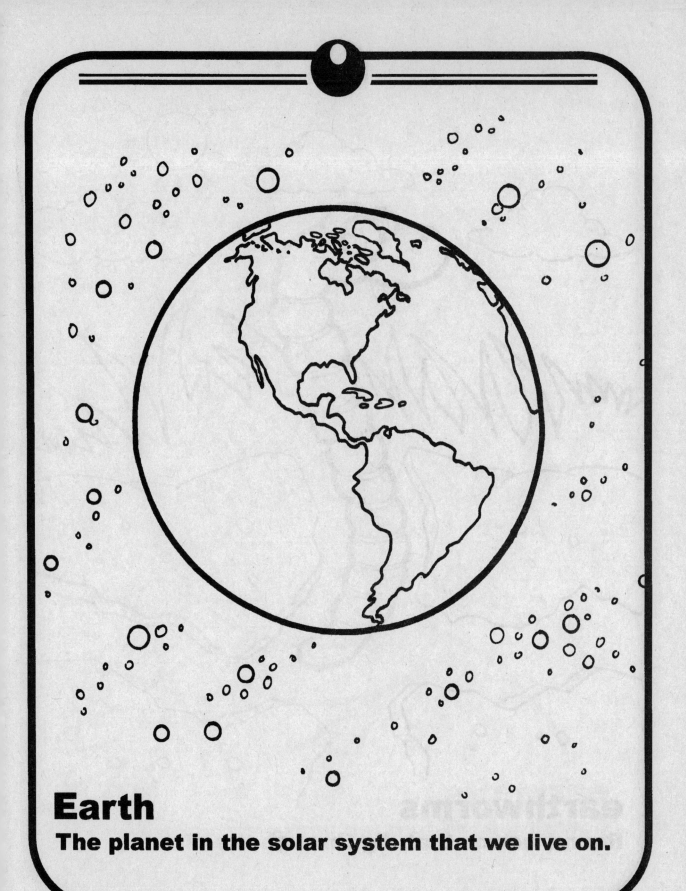

Earth
The planet in the solar system that we live on.

earthworms
Round worms that dig through the dirt.

Easter eggs
Eggs that have been decorated for Easter.

farmer

Someone who works on a farm raising animals or growing crops.

fish

A scaly animal that lives in the water and breathes with gills.

flamingo
A large pink tropical bird.

frog
A tailless, web-footed, jumping amphibian.

garden

Flowers or vegetables grown together in one place.

giraffe
An animal with a very long neck and legs.

golf club
Long stick with a large base used for hitting balls while playing golf.

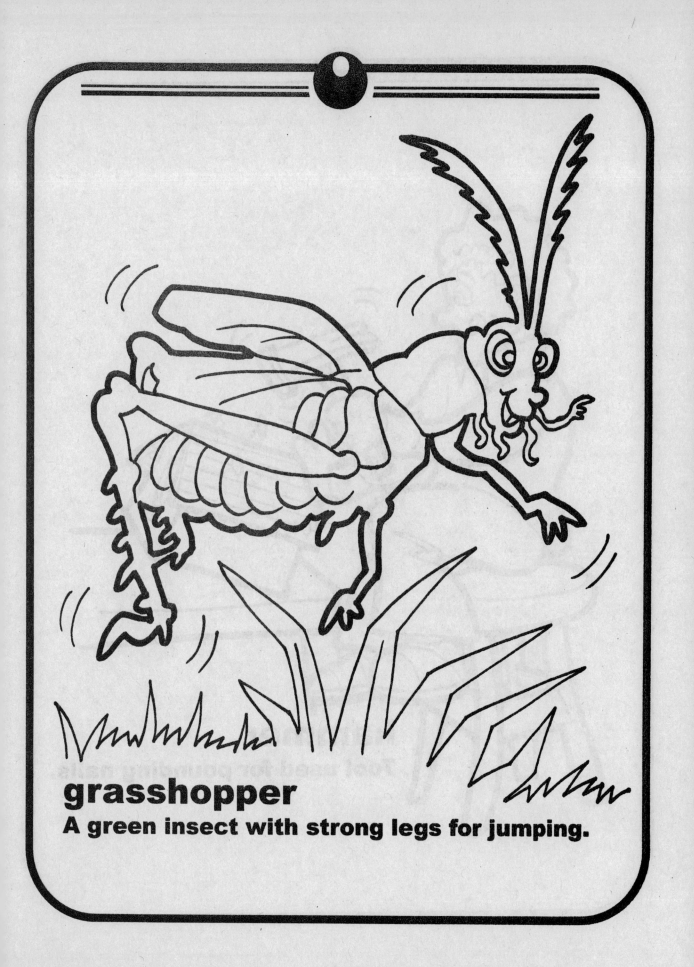

grasshopper
A green insect with strong legs for jumping.

hammer
Tool used for pounding nails.

harp

Large, stringed instrument played with your hands.

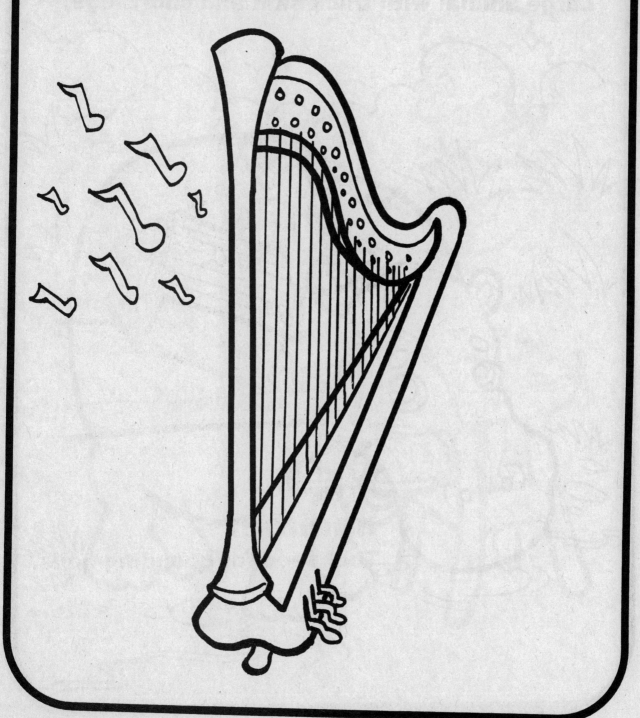

hippopotamus
Large animal with thick skin and short legs.

home
Building where you live.

igloo
Hut built from blocks of snow.

ink bottle
Small bottle used
to hold ink.

island
Piece of land surrounded by water.

jacket
A short coat.

jack-in-the-box
**Musical toy that, when wound,
a doll pops out of a box.**

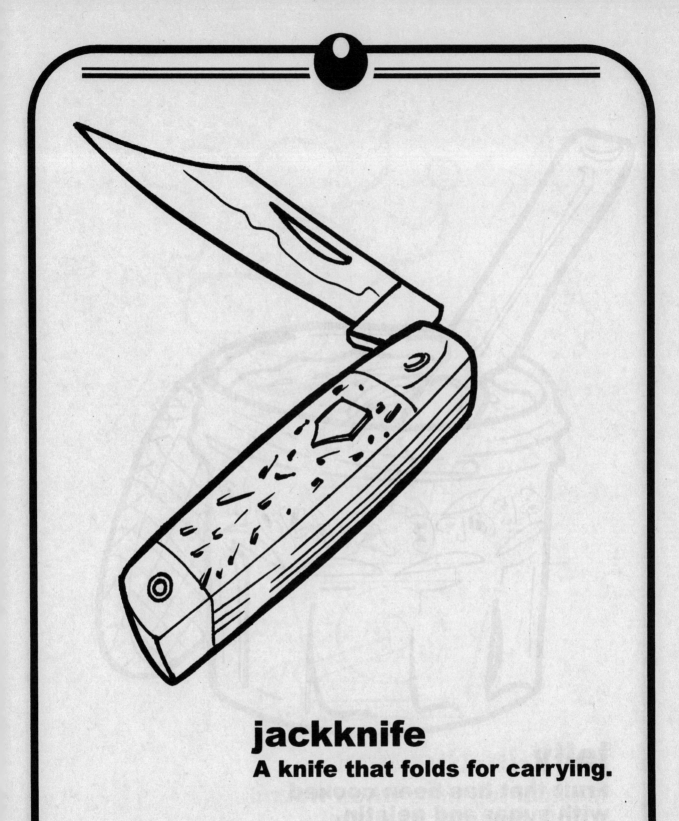

jackknife
A knife that folds for carrying.

jelly
Fruit that has been cooked with sugar and gelatin.

kangaroo

A mammal with short front legs and large hind legs for jumping. The female has a pouch on her front for carrying her young.

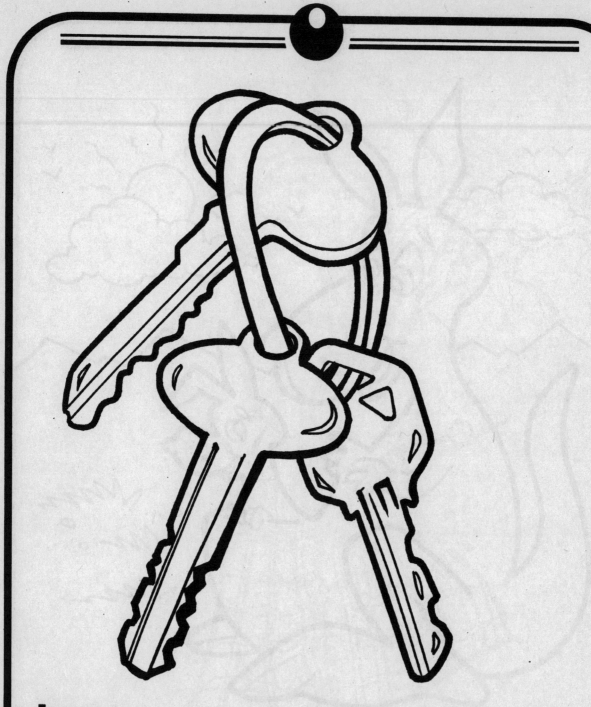

keys
Objects used for unlocking something.

kilt
A pleated skirt.

knight
A military servant to the king.

ladybugs
Small red beetles that have black spotted backs.

lamb
A baby sheep.

leaves

Parts of plants and trees that grow at the end of the branches.

lighthouse
A tall building that uses a bright light to guide ships.

mailbox
A container used
for holding mail.

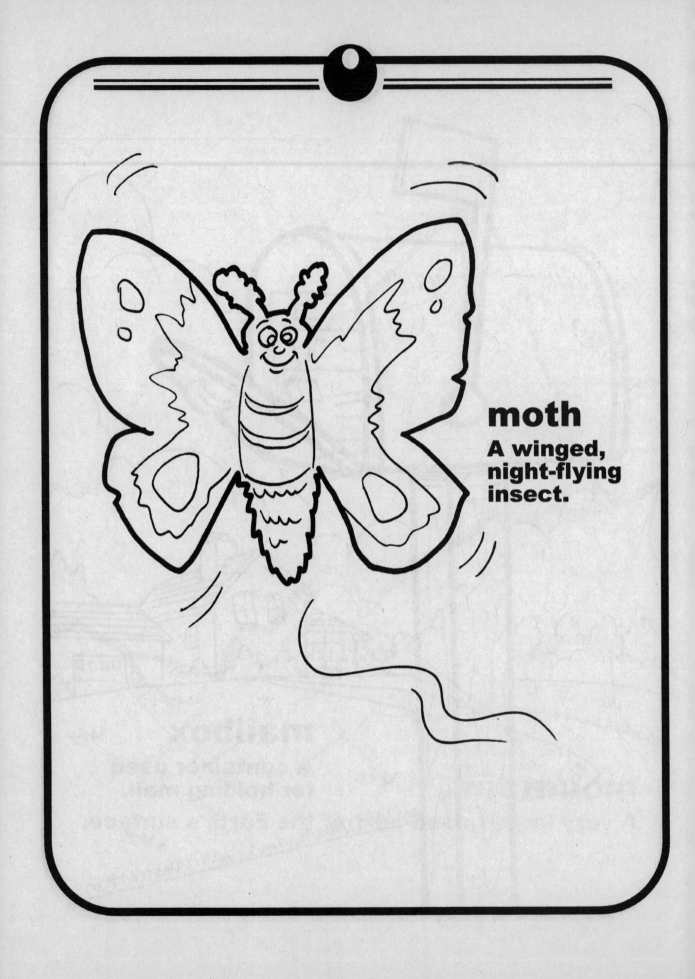

moth
A winged, night-flying insect.

mountain

A very large raised part of the Earth's surface.

muffins
A quick bread that is baked in a shaped cup.

mushroom
A fungus that has a stem and a cap.

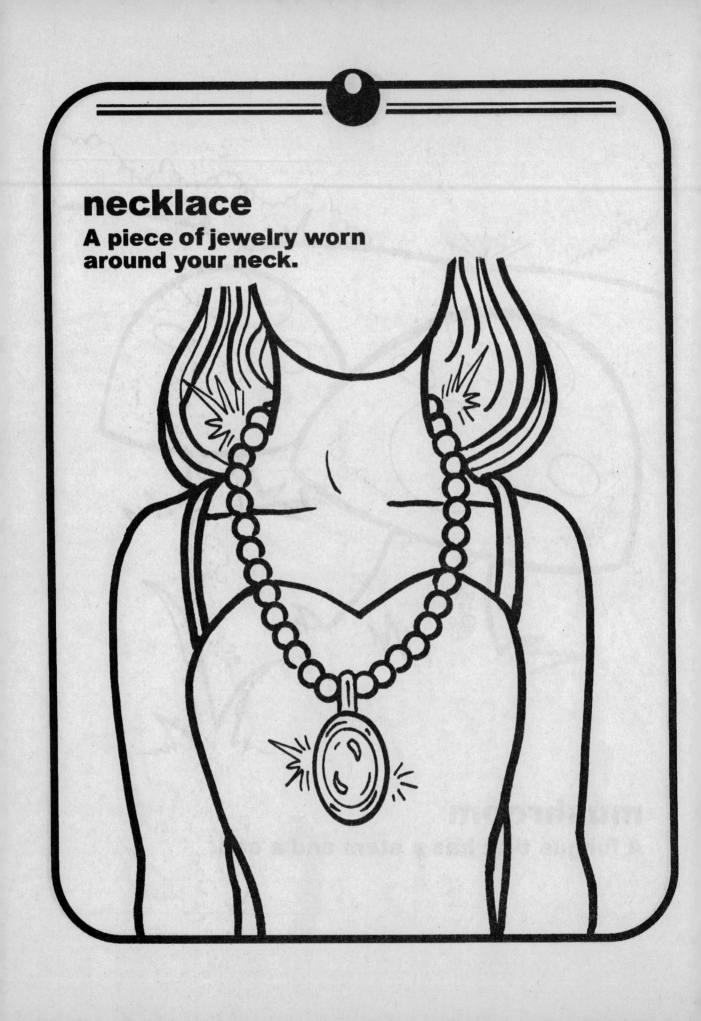

necklace
A piece of jewelry worn around your neck.

notes
Musical symbols.

nut
An edible seed of a plant or tree that usually has a hard shell.

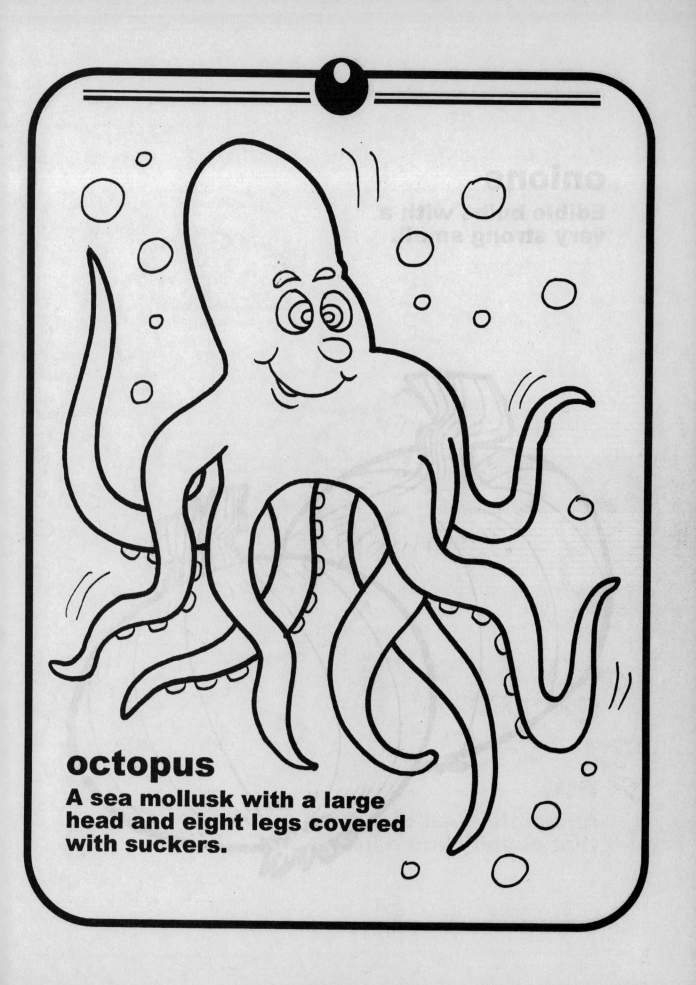

octopus

A sea mollusk with a large head and eight legs covered with suckers.

onions

Edible bulbs with a very strong smell.

ornaments
Decorations used for trimming a tree.

ostrich

A large bird with a long neck and powerful legs for running very fast.

owl
A night bird with large eyes and a flat face.

paintbrush
An instrument used for painting.

pancakes

Flat cakes of batter that are grilled.

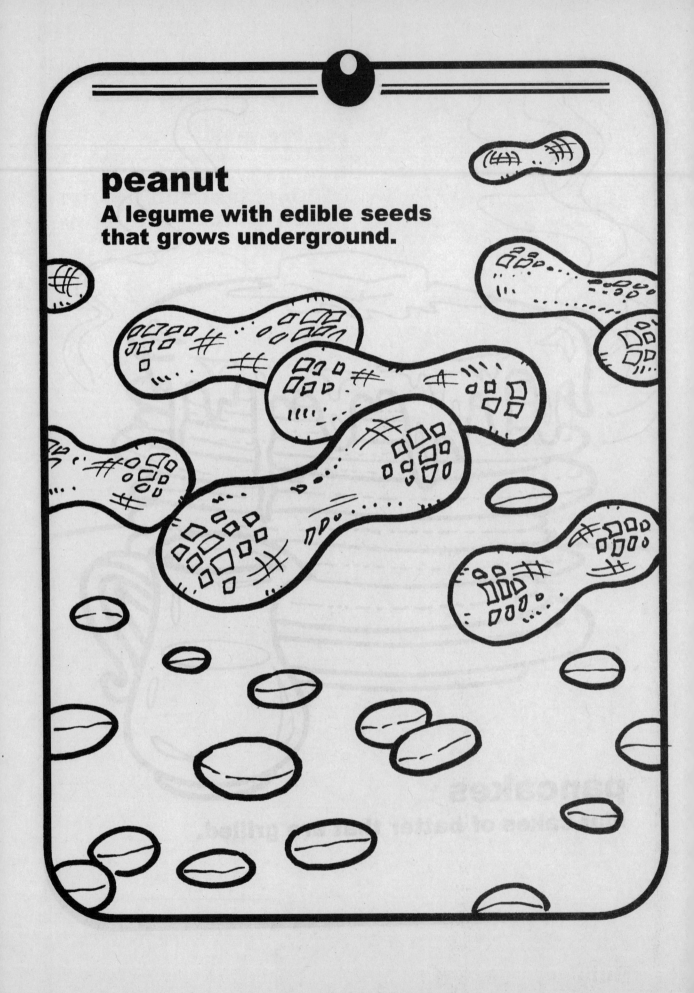

peanut
A legume with edible seeds that grows underground.

pelican

A large water bird with webbed feet and a large pouch on the bottom of its bill.

quail
A small game bird.

queen
A woman who rules a monarchy.

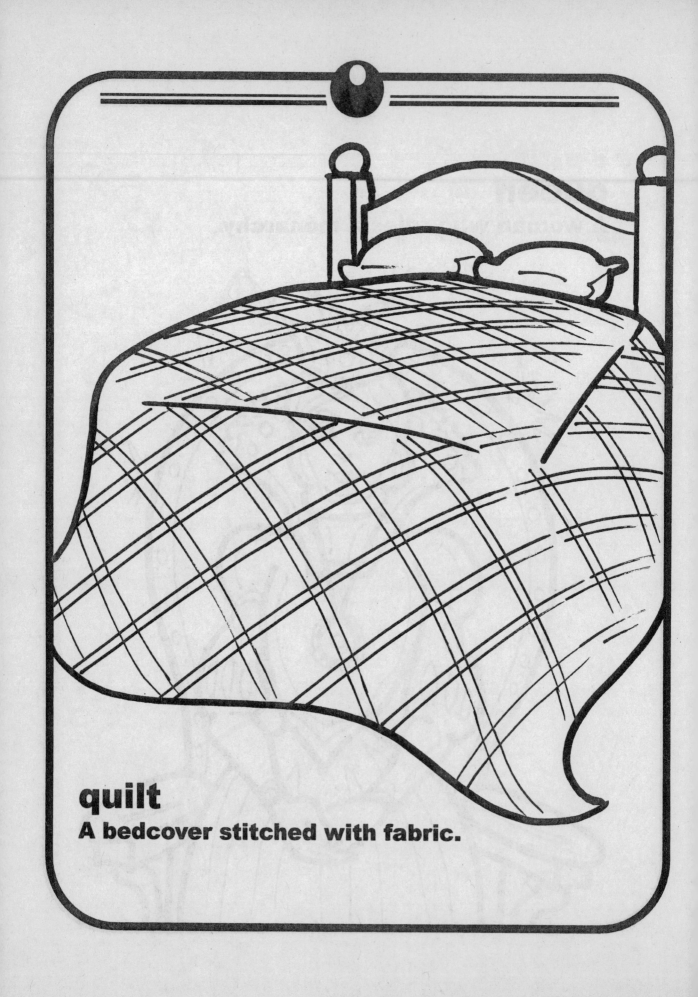

quilt
A bedcover stitched with fabric.

rabbit

A small animal with large ears, a bushy tail and large back legs for hopping.

raccoon

A night animal that has a striped tail and looks like it is wearing a mask.

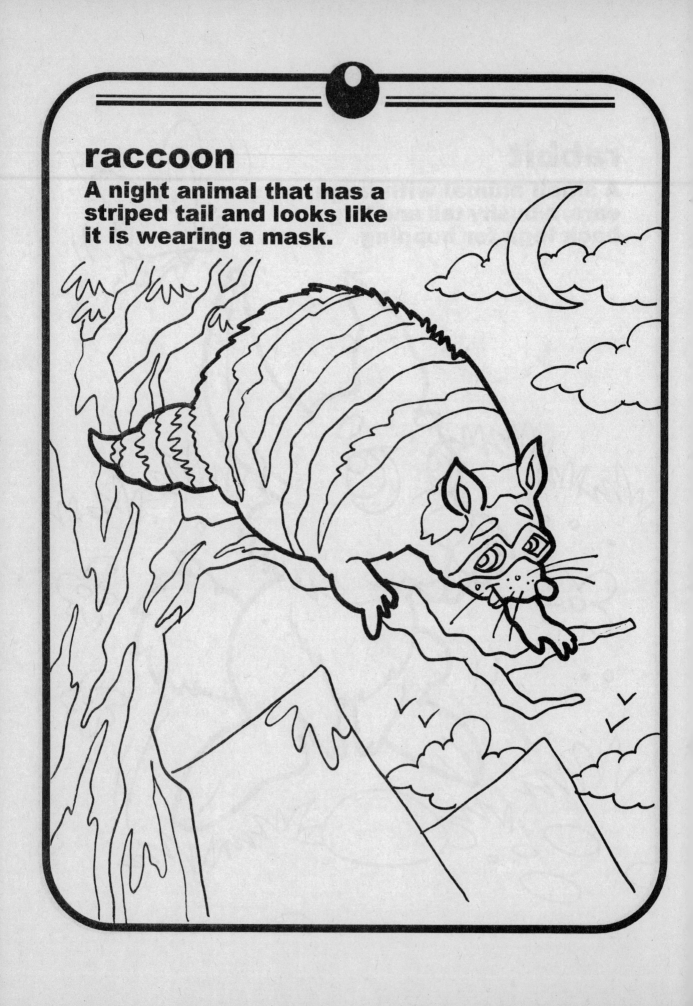

racket

A round frame with strings that is attached to a handle.

rattle
A baby's toy.

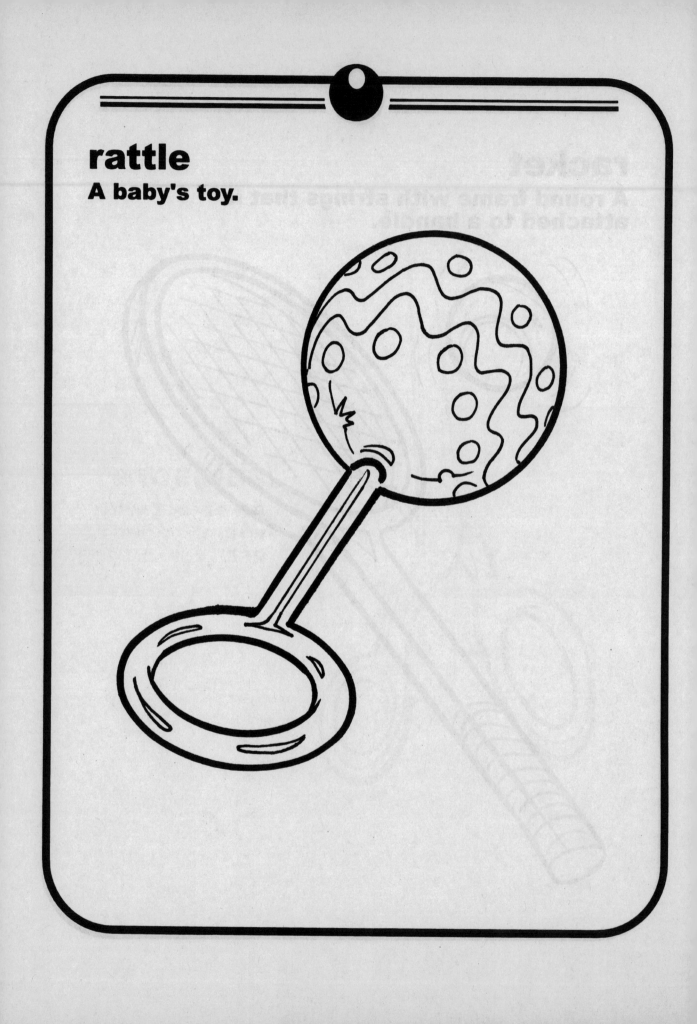

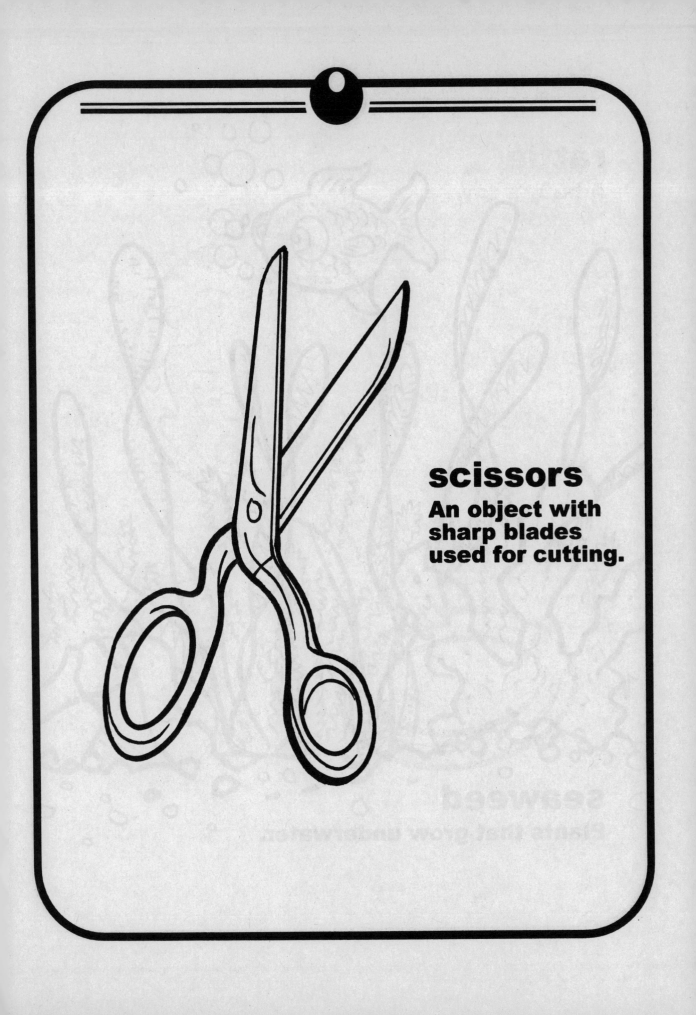

scissors
An object with sharp blades used for cutting.

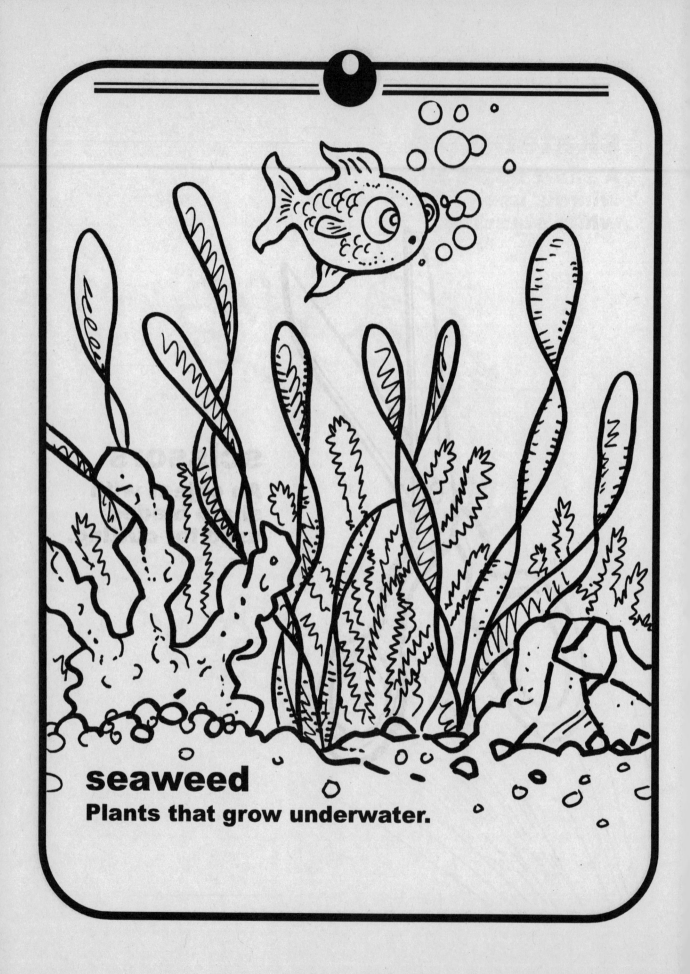

seaweed
Plants that grow underwater.

skateboard

A short board with wheels used for riding while standing.

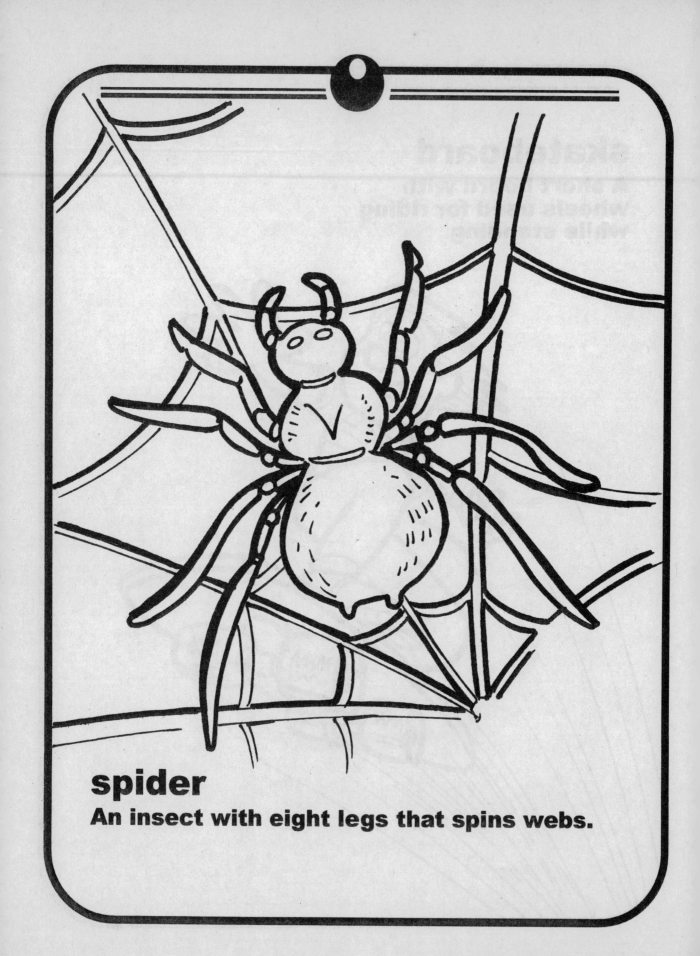

spider
An insect with eight legs that spins webs.

teapot
**A pot that has a handle
and spout used for pouring tea.**

tie
A piece of fabric tied and worn around the neck.

toaster
An appliance used for toasting bread.

tomatoes
Juicy red or yellow fruit that grows on a vine.

tooth
One of the hard, bonelike objects in a mouth used for chewing.

umbrella
A frame covered
with fabric that is
used for protection
from rain or sun.

underwear
Garments that are worn under clothing.

unicorn
A mythical horselike creature that had one horn growing from the center of its forehead.

vase
A container used to hold flowers.

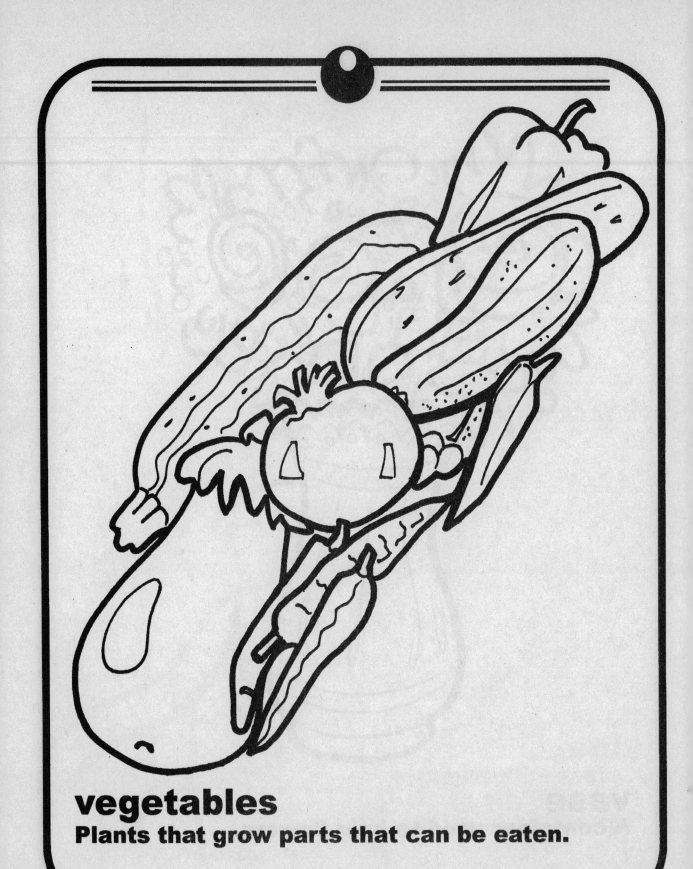

vegetables
Plants that grow parts that can be eaten.

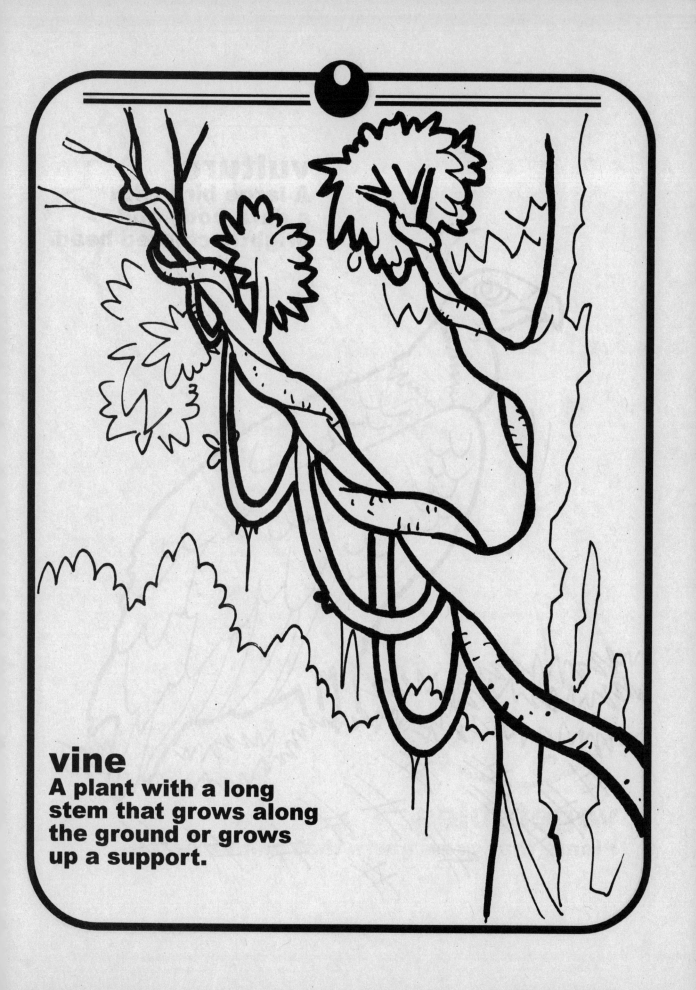

vine
A plant with a long stem that grows along the ground or grows up a support.

vulture
A large bird with
a dark body and
brightly colored head.

wasp
A flying insect that stings.

watermelon
A large fruit with a hard green rind and red, juicy center.

wind chimes
A cluster of hanging objects that make noise when they strike each other.

windmill
A large mill operated by wind rotating blades on the outside.

wolf
A gray doglike animal
that lives in the wild.

x-ray
A way to take pictures of inside something.

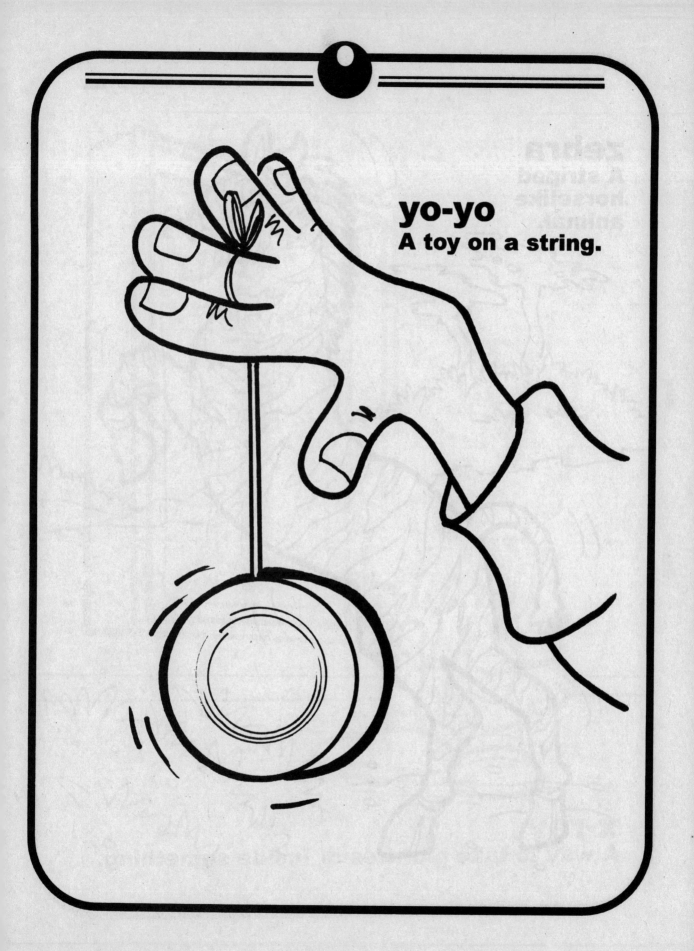

yo-yo
A toy on a string.

zebra
A striped horselike animal.